EGYPTIAN MYTHOLOGY

HATHOR

BY HEATHER C. HUDAK

CONTENT CONSULTANT
KASIA SZPAKOWSKA, PhD
PROFESSOR EMERITUS OF EGYPTOLOGY

Kids Core

An Imprint of Abdo Publishing
abdobooks.com

abdobooks.com

Printed in the United States of America, North Mankato, Minnesota.
052022
092022

THIS BOOK CONTAINS RECYCLED MATERIALS

Cover Photos: Olga Chernyak/Shutterstock Images, Hathor; Shutterstock Images, pyramids
Interior Photos: Christine Osborne Pictures/Alamy, 4–5; Luis Martinez/Shutterstock Images, 6; Unai Huizi Photography/Shutterstock Images, 9; Vladimir Zadvinskii/Shutterstock Images, 10, 28 (bottom); Funkyfood London/Paul Williams/Alamy, 12–13; Peter Horree/Alamy, 14, 23, 28 (top); Liudmila Klymenko/Shutterstock Images, 16, 29 (top); Art Directors & Trip/Alamy, 18; Shutterstock Images, 20–21, 24 (woman), 24 (bust); Marta Jonina/Shutterstock Images, 24 (cow); Akimov Konstantin/Shutterstock Images, 26, 29 (bottom)

Editor: Layna Darling
Series Designer: Ryan Gale

Library of Congress Control Number: 2021952325

Publisher's Cataloging-in-Publication Data

Names: Hudak, Heather C., author.
Title: Hathor / by Heather C. Hudak
Description: Minneapolis, Minnesota : Abdo Publishing, 2023 | Series: Egyptian mythology | Includes online resources and index.
Identifiers: ISBN 9781532198663 (lib. bdg.) | ISBN 9781644947746 (pbk.) | ISBN 9781098272319 (ebook)
Subjects: LCSH: Hathor (Egyptian deity)--Juvenile literature. | Egypt--Religion--Juvenile literature. | Gods, Egyptian--Juvenile literature. | Mythology, Egyptian--Juvenile literature.
Classification: DDC 932.01--dc23

CONTENTS

Hathor, *left*, protected her father, Ra, *right*.

CHAPTER 1

DEFENDER OF RA

Hathor was the daughter of the Sun god Ra. Ra was the king of all gods. All people worshipped and loved him. But Ra began to grow old and weak. People started to wonder if he was strong enough to rule their world. Ra heard what they were saying about him.

Hathor took on the form of a lioness to protect Ra. This sculpture of a lion can be found outside the Temple of Hathor in Egypt.

He became very upset. He decided to teach them a lesson. Hathor was his protector. He asked her to make everyone afraid.

Hathor wanted to help Ra. She took on the form of a lioness and set off to scare the people of Earth. But Hathor was too harsh. She began to destroy Ra's kingdom and hurt people. Ra told her to stop. He still wanted to rule over Earth. Hathor was out of control and wanted to do more damage.

Ra decided to trick Hathor. He made a special red drink and poured it over a field.

Eye of Ra

Hathor was born from one of Ra's tears. Egyptians knew her as the Eye of Ra. She is often shown with the Sun above her head. The Sun represents Ra and Hathor's connection to him. As the Eye of Ra, Hathor protects and defends Ra.

When Hathor saw the pool of liquid, she stopped and stared. Then she drank from it. The brew made her very sleepy. When Hathor awoke, she was kind and happy. She no longer wanted to destroy all people.

Ancient Egypt

Ancient Egypt was a mighty civilization. It was built about 5,000 years ago in northeastern Africa. It lasted more than 3,000 years. Ancient Egyptians left behind many clues about their ways of life, including buildings, artwork, and myths.

Ancient Egyptians wanted to understand the world around them. They told stories to explain the world and how it came to be.

Temples that still stand today give clues about the ancient Egyptians' ways of life.

Hathor was one of the most well-known
Egyptian goddesses.

These are known as Egyptian myths. Gods and goddesses were a big part of Egyptian myths. They had special powers and could perform incredible acts.

Hathor was one of the most important goddesses. She was the goddess of motherhood and fertility. Hathor was worshipped by people from all parts of ancient Egypt.

Further Evidence

Look at the website below. Does it give any new evidence to support Chapter One?

Ancient Egypt

abdocorelibrary.com/hathor

Hathor, *left*, was seen as a protector of pharaohs. She is pictured here with Seti I, *right*, who ruled Egypt from 1290 to 1279 BCE.

CHAPTER 2

KIND AND GIVING GODDESS

Hathor had a cruel and bloodthirsty side to her. But she was known mainly for her kind and loving nature. She was worshipped as a protector of pharaohs and mothers. She helped women become pregnant and have children.

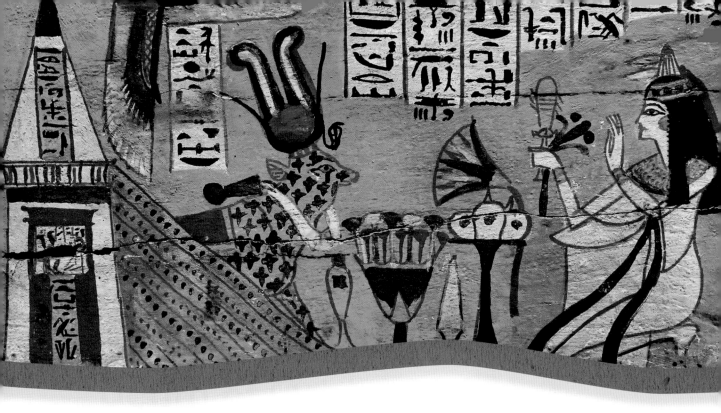

Hathor, *pictured here as a cow*, welcomed people into the afterlife.

She also protected women as they gave birth. Hathor watched over their children.

Hathor brought people into the world at birth. She also helped them enter the next world when they died. In this way, Hathor was a caretaker of both the living and the dead. Ancient Egyptians saw death on Earth as the start of life in the next world. Hathor provided food and hope to the souls of the dead when they reached the afterlife. The afterlife was where ancient Egyptians thought a person's soul went after death. Hathor welcomed people into this place.

Goddess of Many Names

Hathor was one of the first ancient Egyptian goddesses. She was known as the Mother Goddess. She cared for all life on Earth. Hathor was also known as the goddess of the sky, love, joy, music, and dance. She protected the people of Egypt. Hathor had power over anything to do with women. She oversaw their health, beauty, and matters of the heart.

The goddess Isis was known for protection and motherhood, like Hathor.

Over time, ancient Egyptians changed the roles of their gods and goddesses. Gods took on new powers and lost others. Sometimes, different gods were blended into one. Myths about the gods didn't always match up with their current roles. Hathor's role changed often. She was known as the goddess of many names.

Hathor was often called the Mother of Mothers or the Eye of Ra. She was closely linked to many other goddesses, such as Sekhmet and Isis.

Hathor and Horus

In some myths, Hathor was the mother of Horus. In other myths, Hathor was Horus's wife. Horus was an important god. Egypt's pharaoh was thought to represent Horus on Earth.

Hathor and Isis

Isis was the goddess of fertility, healing, rebirth, and magic. She had many of the same powers and roles as Hathor. It is often hard to tell them apart in Egyptian myths and art. Like Hathor, Isis is often seen with horns. She also has been shown with a headdress similar to Hathor's.

Hathor, *left*, was known as a protector of pharaohs like Menkaure, *center*.

The pharaoh had total power over his kingdom. He served as a link between his people and the gods.

Hathor represented the mother or wife of Egypt's pharaohs. In both roles, she served as their protector. She defended Horus and gave him advice. Queens on Earth did the same with their pharaohs. The queen was a **symbol** of Hathor on Earth.

Many Egyptians worshipped Hathor. This hymn, or song, to Hathor is found at the Temple of Medamud in Egypt. Part of it goes:

> The whole world rejoices to you,
>
> the animals dance for you in joy,
>
> the Two Lands and the foreign countries
>
> praise you.

Source: John Coleman Darnell. *Hathor Returns to Medamud.* Academia, 1995. 93.

Comparing Texts

Think about the quote. Does it support the information in this chapter? Or does it give a different perspective? Explain how in a few sentences.

Hathor was beloved across Egypt. This statue of her is found outside her temple in Dendera, Egypt.

CHAPTER 3

WORSHIPPED BY ALL

Some gods and goddesses were worshipped only in certain parts of Egypt. But Hathor was beloved across Egypt. Everyone worshipped her. Ancient Egyptians asked Hathor to protect them in life and death.

They also talked to Hathor about their problems and asked her to bless them.

Celebrating Hathor

Hathor gave many gifts to the people of Earth. Ancient Egyptians believed she nourished all life. Artwork of Hathor often shows her as a provider. She was sometimes represented as a cow or as a woman with a cow's head or ears.

Goddess of Beauty

Hathor was the goddess of beauty and makeup. Cosmetics were popular in ancient Egyptian culture. Women would leave Hathor gifts of mirrors and makeup.

Ancient Egyptians thought cows were giving creatures. Because of this, Hathor is often shown as a cow.

Hathor in Her Main Forms

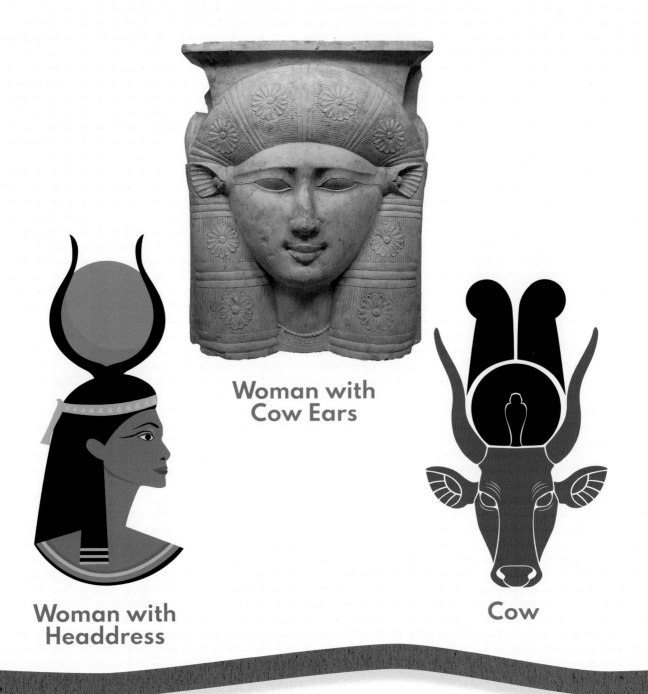

Woman with Cow Ears

Woman with Headdress

Cow

Hathor is shown in mainly three different forms. She can be seen as a woman wearing a headdress, a woman with cow ears, or a cow.

Cows were seen as giving creatures because of their milk. They nourished the ancient Egyptians. Showing Hathor as a cow symbolized how she was a provider.

More than 2,000 years ago, the ancient Egyptians built a temple to honor Hathor in Dendera, Egypt. The Temple of Hathor was a place to worship the goddess. Ancient Egyptians worshipped her by dancing and singing. They also left offerings to her. People believed she would travel there each year around summer, at the start of the great Nile River floods. The floods fertilized the land, helping grow new life. The temple still stands today.

Ancient Egyptians worshipped the goddess at the
Temple of Hathor in Dendera.

Hathor was widely celebrated. More festivals honored Hathor than any other god or goddess. Ancient Egyptians held a festival honoring her birthday every year at her temple. It was called the Hathor Festival. Many ancient Egyptians gathered to sing, dance, and drink to honor the goddess. Hathor was loved all across Egypt.

Explore Online

Visit the website below. Does it give any new information about the Temple of Hathor that wasn't in Chapter Three?

Dendera Complex Temple

abdocorelibrary.com/hathor

LEGENDARY FACTS

Hathor could be cruel and punishing. But she also could be kind and giving.

Hathor was the goddess of love, women, fertility, joy, music, dance, and beauty. She was also the goddess of the sky.

Hathor shared many roles with the goddess Isis. They even look alike in Egyptian art.

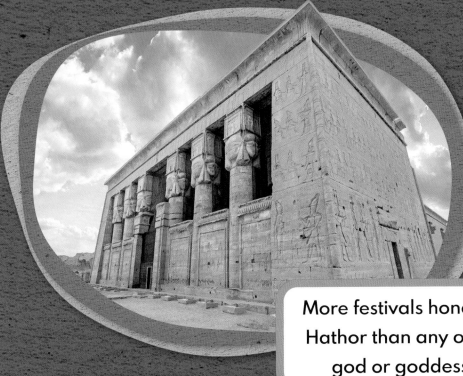

More festivals honored Hathor than any other god or goddess.

Glossary

afterlife
in ancient Egypt, a place where a person's spirit goes after death

civilization
a complex, organized society

fertility
the ability to create life and support growth

nourished
to have given people food and other things they need to live healthy lives

pharaoh
the ruler of an Egyptian kingdom; the king

symbol
an object that represents a certain quality or idea

Online Resources

To learn more about Hathor, visit our free resource websites below.

Visit **abdocorelibrary.com** or scan this QR code for free Common Core resources for teachers and students, including vetted activities, multimedia, and booklinks, for deeper subject comprehension.

Visit **abdobooklinks.com** or scan this QR code for free additional online weblinks for further learning. These links are routinely monitored and updated to provide the most current information available.

Learn More

Alexander, Heather. *A Child's Introduction to Egyptology.* Black Dog & Leventhal, 2021.

Gieseke, Tyler. *Egyptian Gods and Goddesses.* Abdo, 2022.

Index

About the Author

Heather C. Hudak has written hundreds of kids' books on all kinds of topics. She loves to travel when she's not writing. Hudak has visited about 60 countries and hopes to travel to Egypt one day. She also enjoys camping with her husband and many pets.